Let's Dough It Again

by Paulette S. Jarvey

Printed in the United States of America
Library of Congress

First printing, December 1980
Second printing, April 1981
Third printing, November 1981
Fourth printing, October 1982
Fifth printing, March 1983
Sixth printing, December 1983
Seventh printing, September 1984
Eighth printing, May 1985
Ninth printing, December 1985
Tenth printing, September 1986
Eleventh printing, February 1987
Twelfth printing, August 1987
Thirteenth printing, March 1988
Fouteenth printing, November 1988
Fifteenth printing, October 1989
Sixteenth printing, April 1990

Hot Off The Press, Inc., publishing
7212 S Seven Oaks, Dept. B
Canby, Oregon   97013

Contents

4

To my parents, Reva and Charles McCord, who are very tidy, meticulous people. From their daughter who Isn't. With muoh lovo.

edited by Suzanne Kosewick Jones
cover design and line drawings by Dave Jones
page layout by Ruth Rodgers
title by John T. Kosewick
proof reading, paste-up, and "About the Author" by Joan Humbert
black and white photographs by Mike Jarvey
cover photographed by Bill Werts Photography, Los Angeles, California.

Dough art is an inexpensive, versatile, and easy craft.

Is it necessary to have YOU CAN DOUGH IT! to understand LET'S DOUGH IT AGAIN? No. Each book is written to stand alone (although I would appreciate it if you had them both!). This book is an extension of the first one with more designs and some new techniques. After ten years of designing, making, selling, and teaching dough art, I still really enjoy this craft. It is so satisfying to take a lump of dough and turn it into a funny dragon or a sweet little bear. And yes, you can do the same. All projects are broken down into easy step-by-step photographs and instructions. Relax and have fun.

One note, the designs in this book are for you to make for your personal use or gifts. All pieces are copyrighted and no one may legally sell them without my written permission. However, the book may be used for classes. If you would like additional copies of LET'S DOUGH IT AGAIN or YOU CAN DOUGH IT! please check your local book or craft store. Or, you may order by writing to me at Hot Off the Press. Once again, I sincerely hope you enjoy doing dough.

DOUGH ART RECIPE

There are many but this is the best! Measure carefully.

> 4 cups flour
> 1 cup plain or iodized salt
> 1½ cups hot water (as it comes from the tap)

> 1. Pour the hot water and salt into a bowl and stir for 1 minute. The grains of salt will reduce in size but not dissolve.

> 2. Add the flour and stir until the water is absorbed. (It is a good idea to remove your rings before the next step.)

> 3. Turn the dough onto a table or bread board and knead a few minutes. The dough is ready when it is smooth and pliable.

> 4. Keep the dough in a plastic bag so it will not dry out as you use it.

This recipe may be cut in half or increased by doubling or tripling the ingredients. It is best to use the dough within 24 hours. Left over dough should be stored without refrigeration in a plastic bag.

MIXING

TEXTURE OF DOUGH

- Too sticky: knead in more flour, however, the dough will remain soft.
- Too dry: moisten your fingers with water and continue to knead. If necessary, place the dough in a plastic bag and sprinkle with a few drops of water. Then set the dough aside for ½ hour.

TYPES OF FLOUR

- Bleached or unbleached flour works best.
- Do not use self-rising flour.
- Whole wheat and rye flours are not very satisfactory. They do not make as smooth and pliable a dough as white flour.

TO ADD COLOR

- For a bright color that does not fade, use liquid tempera paint.
- Put ¼ cup liquid tempera paint into a measuring cup and add hot water until the total liquid is 1⅔ cups. Notice that this is more liquid than the basic recipe requires. Mix as usual.
- Food coloring, dry mustard, paprika, liquid coffee or tea can also be added to the hot water. The total liquid should be 1½ cups.

SHAPING

JOINING TWO PIECES OF DOUGH

- Where dough touches dough it must be joined with water. Since water is used frequently, keep some nearby when working with dough.

THE USE OF ALUMINUM FOIL

- For each project you will be told when to place the dough onto a sheet of aluminum foil. When ready to bake, simply lift the foil and transfer it to the cookie sheet. The foil prevents the dough from sticking to the cookie sheet.
- Aluminum foil is also shaped into a form. Then dough is placed over the form to make larger, thicker projects. See page 29.

TOOLS

- Most tools needed for dough art can be found in the kitchen. The basic tools include: cookie sheet, aluminum foil, rolling pin, knife, straw, nutpick, and garlic press.
- For your convenience, each project has a list of tools "you will need."

GLAZING

The directions for each project will tell which glaze is to be applied to that project.

- Egg white, evaporated milk or mayonnaise is applied before baking. Each gives a shiny, light brown glaze.
- Egg yolk is painted on with a small paint brush. Apply it before baking for a dark brown glaze.
- For a vivid color mix food coloring in evaporated milk and paint before baking.
- Plastic cooking crystals can be used for a "stained glass" effect. Position them just before baking.
- Poppy seeds, sesame seeds, caraway seeds, mustard seeds all give an interesting textured glaze. Spread egg white on the dough before sprinkling on the seeds.

BAKING

WHEN TO BAKE

- Bake as soon as your project is made. If it is not possible to bake immediately, cover the dough with plastic until you can bake.
- Providing the oven temperature is as required for the dough, foods can be baked in the oven with dough art.

TEMPERATURE

- Bake at 325°. Most projects will take 1 to 4 hours to bake. Estimates for baking time follow each project in this book.
- Thin projects should be baked at 300° to prevent the dough from "puffing" up.
- Dough art over a form, i.e., bread baskets, jar lid covers, and napkin rings should be baked at 250°, and allowed to cool slowly.

TESTING FOR DONENESS

- When the dough is hard all over it is done. Test by pressing at the thickest part. If there is any give, continue baking.
- If baked too long, the dough will burn.

MICROWAVE

- Using a microwave is not recommended, because the dough turns white, instead of golden brown. However, if you do use one, please read on.
- Do not use aluminum foil or make any project with a foil form or a wire hook.
- Thin dough art projects can be baked in a microwave at a low temperature, if turned often.

AIR DRY

- Dough art cannot be successfully air dried. It cracks and crumbles too easily.

CHANGE IN SIZE AND SHAPE

- Usually there is no significant change in the size of a project. Occasionally, a thin piece of dough will lift up. If this happens, weigh the piece down with an oven proof pan. Next time lower the baking temperature 25°.
- If a project "puffs up" during baking, also weigh it down with an oven proof pan. Again, lower the baking temperature by 25°, next time.

FINISHING

PAINT

- Use acrylic, watercolor, poster, tempera or model paints.
- Oil-based paints take too long to dry.
- Use a felt-tip pen for detail work, then use a spray fix before sealing.

GLUE

- To attach dough to a board use a brand of craft glue that will dry clear and remain flexible.
- Silicone glue will also work but it is expensive.
- Allow the glue to dry 24 hours before hanging up the project.
- Flowers, ribbons, and rick rack can be attached effectively with most any type of glue.

SEAL

- All dough art must be sealed. A gloss acrylic spray works very well. Use several coats of spray to thoroughly seal the dough. If the dough project is glued onto a board, spray it after gluing. Always spray outside because of harmful fumes.
- Varathane, shellac, varnish, or even clear fingernail polish will also seal the dough.
- Christmas ornaments, projects handled frequently, and projects placed in a room with high moisture, must be thoroughly sealed. A polymer coating works very well.
- A product called "Joli Glaze" is an excellent sealer. Be sure to use two coats for the best protection.

Strawberries in a Basket

Strawberries are colorful, easy to make, and quite versatile.
For a new look, stretch fabric over an embroidery hoop
and use a craft glue to attach the dough. Then glue
a few sprigs of baby's breath behind the berries. Or attach
the piece to a board or straw mat. Without a basket, the
berries and blossoms are attractive around the edge of a
recipe box or on a board with a strawberry huller. Use
red-colored dough to make the berries, otherwise paint them
after baking. Apples, lemons, blueberries, and oranges
work well in this basket. Directions for them follow.

YOU WILL NEED:

rolling pin
knife
nutpick
unlined paper (lined paper
  bleeds onto the dough)
pencil, scissors
aluminum foil
water
for apples and oranges—cloves

basket pattern

1 batch of dough will make
8 strawberries in a basket

1   Trace the basket pattern on unlined paper and cut it out. Roll out a pancake of dough ¼" thick. Cut out the basket.

2   With a knife press in lines. Do not cut through the dough.

At this point transfer the basket to a sheet of aluminum foil.

1

2

3   Make a foil ball the size of a grape. Place on the table and press to flatten the ball. Insert it under the center of the basket.

4   Roll out a pancake of dough ¼" thick. Cut two strips each ¼" wide and 3" long.

3

4

5   Moisten the back of each strip and place on the basket as shown. Cut off the excess length.

6   With the blunt end of a nutpick make indentations along each strip.

5

6

7   To make a strawberry: take a ball of dough the size of a grape. Roll between your palms until smooth.

8   Slightly pinch one end of the ball.

7

8

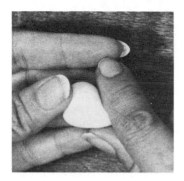

9

10

9 Gently flatten the opposite end of the ball.

10 Dab water on the back of the berry and place on the basket. Repeat until the basket is full of strawberries.

11

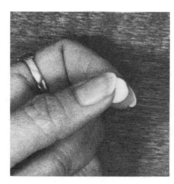

12

11 With the curved end of a nutpick press indentations for seeds. Notice that the nutpick is flat against the berry.

12 For leaves (the calyx): roll a very small ball of dough the size of a pea. Flatten the ball between your fingers.

13

14

13 Pinch one end to a point.

14 Put a drop of water on the top of a berry and attach the leaf. Make more leaves and place as shown.

Bake at 325° until hard, about 2½ hours.

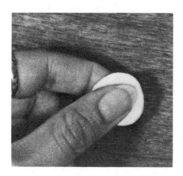

15

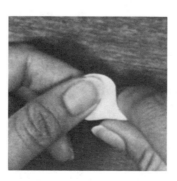

16

15 To make strawberry blossoms: roll a ball of dough the size of a marble. Flatten the ball between your fingers.

16 Pinch one end to a point.

14

17

18

17 Make another petal. Dip the pointed end in water and place next to the first petal. Repeat until there are five petals. Roll a tiny ball for the center and join with water. After baking the center should be painted yellow.

18 To make an apple: use a ball of dough the size of a grape. Roll it between your palms until smooth.

19

20

19 For the stem: press in a clove as shown.

20 Press another clove into the opposite end of the apple. Note: if the clove has a seed, remove it.

21

22

21 For apple leaves: see steps 12 to 14.

22 To make a lemon: take a lump of dough the size of a grape and roll until smooth. Place on the table and gently pinch both ends. Lemon leaves are made like strawberry leaves.

23

24

23 Blueberries are made with small balls of dough piled on top of each other. Make their leaves like the strawberry's.

24 Oranges are made from a lump of dough the size of a grape. After the dough is smooth gently roll the ball over a dry towel to create the texture of an orange. Add leaves. Press in cloves as for apples.

I Hate Housework!

This plaque reflects my personal feelings about housework! Of course, the banner can be changed—try "A Woman's Work Is Never Done." Or personalize the piece with "World's Greatest Grandma" or "For Our Super Scout Leader." After baking, use a black felt-tip pen with a fine point to write your message on the banner. Paint the apron and glue on matching rick rack for a color coordinated look. To further personalize the piece, glue a miniature mop, skillet, or gardening trowel in the hands after the piece is baked.

YOU WILL NEED:

garlic press
rolling pin
knife
aluminum foil
water

1 batch of dough will
make 8 pieces

1

2

1   To make the head: roll a ball of dough the size of a walnut between your palms until smooth.

2   Gently flatten the ball with your fingers until it is ½" thick.

Place the head on a sheet of aluminum foil.

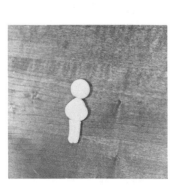

3

4

3   For the body: roll until smooth another ball of dough the size of a walnut. Gently flatten until it is ¼" thick.

4   Place the body on the table and pinch one end. Gently flatten until it is a little thinner than the head.

5

6

5   Dip the pinched end in water and place below the head.

6   For the legs: take a lump of dough the size of a walnut. Roll a coil as thin as a pencil.

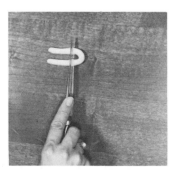

7

8

7   Bring the rounded ends together. Cut so each leg is 1½" long.

8   Put water between the legs and join together. Dip the cut ends in water and attach them to the body.

9

10

11

12

13

14

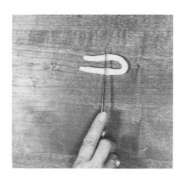

15

16

9 Pinch up the feet as shown.

10 For the dress: trace the basket pattern from page 11 onto unlined paper and cut out. Roll a pancake of dough 1/8'' thick. Cut out the dress.

11 Moisten the back of the dress with water and position it on the body as shown. Pinch up the ends of the dress for a slight flair.

12 For the apron: roll out a pancake of dough 1/8'' thick. Cut a rectangle 1'' x 1½'' and a ¾'' square. Also cut four strips each ¼'' wide and 1'' long.

13 Pick up the rectangle and gather one long edge. Moisten the back with water and place on the girl. Position the square as shown.

14 Put water on the back of two of the strips and place as pictured.

15 For the arms: roll out a coil of dough as thin as a pencil. Place the ends together and cut so each arm is 1'' long.

16 Pinch the cut end of each arm.

17

18

17 Spread water down each arm and place on the girl. Notice the pinched end goes between the head and body. Curve the arms onto the apron.

18 Put water on the other two strips. Lay them over the shoulders to meet the top of the apron.

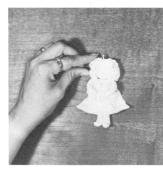

19

20

19 For the hair: moisten the head (not the face). Fill the garlic press with dough and squeeze out ¾".

20 Lift off the hair and place on the head as shown.

21

22

21 Fill the garlic press again and squeeze out ¾" of dough.

22 Repeat for the bangs.

23 For the banner: roll out a pancake of dough ¼" thick. Cut a curved banner 1" wide. Trim the ends as shown.

Bake at 325° until hard, about 1 hour for the banner and 2 hours for the girl.

24 After baking use a black felt-tip pen with a fine point to draw on the face. The addition of slanted eyebrows gives a woeful look. Use a spray fix.

23

24

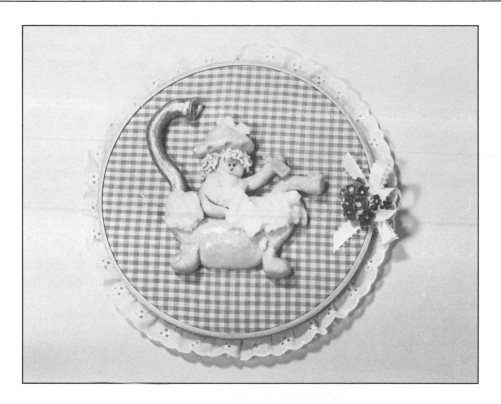

Fun in the Tub

With this project dough art enters another room of your house, the bathroom. After baking, paint the bathtub and shower bonnet a matching color. Use silver model paint to cover the showerhead. Draw the face with a black felt-tip pen with a fine point. Then use a spray fix. It is very important to thoroughly seal this piece because of the moisture in most bathrooms. Follow the directions on page 10 under sealing Christmas ornaments. The "suds" are whipped wax and directions are included.

YOU WILL NEED:

unlined paper (lined paper
  bleeds onto the dough)
pencil, scissors
nutpick
garlic press
rolling pin
knife
aluminum foil
water

paraffin
whip or fork

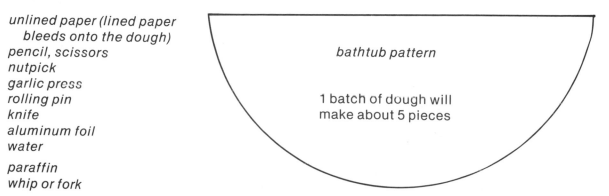

bathtub pattern

1 batch of dough will
make about 5 pieces

1   Trace the bathtub pattern on unlined paper and cut out. Roll a pancake of dough ¼" thick. Cut out one tub.

Place the tub on a sheet of aluminum foil.

2   For the tub feet: roll a coil as thick as your little finger. Bring the ends together and cut so each end is 1" long.

3   Pinch the cut ends. Dip in water and join to the bathtub.

4   For the pipe and showerhead: roll a coil of dough as thick as your little finger. Cut a piece 5" long.

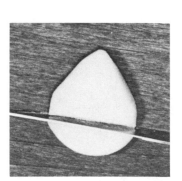

5   Gently pinch around one end to form the showerhead.

6   Dip the other end in water and join to the tub. Curve the coil as shown.

7   For the girl's body: take a lump of dough the size of a walnut. Roll until smooth. Gently flatten until it is ¼" thick.

8   Pinch one end. Cut ½" off the opposite end.

9

10

9 Dip the cut end in water. Join the body to the bathtub.

10 For the head: roll a lump of dough a bit smaller than for the body. Gently press until it is ¼" thick. Join it to the body with water.

11

12

11 For the arms: roll a coil of dough as thin as a pencil. Bring both ends together and cut so each arm is 1½" long.

12 Pinch the cut ends. Spread water on the back of each arm and place as shown.

13

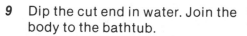

14

13 For the hair: dab water on the head (not on the face). Fill a garlic press with dough. Squeeze out ½".

14 With your finger slide off the dough.

15

16

15 Arrange the hair.

16 For the leg: roll a coil as thin as a pencil. Cut a piece 2" long. The rounded end will be the foot.

17 Dip the cut end in water and join it to the tub.

18 Gently pinch up a foot.

17   **18**

19 For a shower bonnet: roll until smooth a ball of dough the size of a walnut. Press it down over your knuckle.

20 Pinch all around to form a brim.

19   **20**

21 Dab water inside the bonnet. Carefully pick up the girl's head and position the bonnet.

22 With the blunt end of a nutpick press in a ruffle.

Bake at 325° until hard, about 2½ hours. Cool. Paint as desired. Draw on the face. Use a spray fix. Thoroughly seal and glue to fabric stretched over an embroidery hoop.

21   **22**

23 For the suds: put a block of paraffin in a can. Place that can in a pan of water. Heat until the paraffin melts.

24 Remove from the heat. Let the paraffin cool for a few minutes. Then whip with a fork or wire whisk. When frothy spread the wax.

23   **24**

Cowboy

"Yahoo!" This colorful pint-sized cowboy will brighten any child's room. In making this fellow you will follow the basic steps for shaping most dough art people. Then, simply by changing the hat and clothes the cowboy can become a football player, fisherman, soccer player, or whatever you like. After baking the figure, use a black felt-tip pen with a fine point to draw on the face. Then use a spray fix. Paint the clothing, glue the cowboy to a board and seal. The kerchief is a small triangle of gingham and the rope is a piece of heavy twine. For the finishing trim, rick rack is glued around the edge of the board.

YOU WILL NEED:

garlic press
rolling pin
knife   1 batch of dough will
nutpick   make about 6 cowboys
aluminum foil
water

1

2

1   For the head: roll until smooth a ball of dough the size of a walnut. Gently press between your palms until it is ½" thick.

Place the head on a sheet of aluminum foil.

2   For the torso: roll until smooth a ball of dough the size of a walnut. Gently press between your palms until it is a little thinner than the head. Pinch one end.

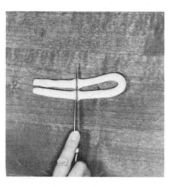

3

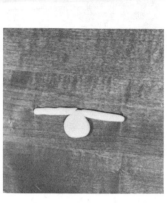

4

3   For the arms: roll a coil of dough as thin as a pencil. Bring the rounded ends together. Cut so each arm is 2" long.

4   Pinch the cut end and join with water to the torso as shown. Spread water over the arms and torso.

5

6

5   For the shirt: roll out a pancake of dough 1/8" thick. Place it over the body as shown.

6   Shape the shirt over the body. Be sure to cover the sides of the torso and arms (not the back). Use a knife to trim off the excess dough. Smooth the cut edges.

7

8

7   Curve the arms as shown. Join the body to the head with water.

8   For the legs: roll out a coil of dough as thick as your little finger. Bring the rounded ends together and cut so each leg is 2" long.

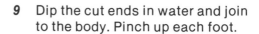

9

10

9 Dip the cut ends in water and join to the body. Pinch up each foot.

10 For the jeans: roll out a pancake of dough 1/8" thick. Cut across the top.

11

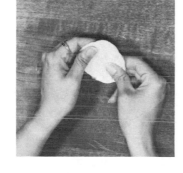

12

11 Position on the cowboy as shown. Shape the jeans over the legs. Be sure to cover the sides of each leg. Trim away the excess dough.

12 Lift off the jeans. Spread water on the back and place. Smooth the cut edges.

13

14

13 For the hair: dab water over the head (not the face). Fill a garlic press with dough. Squeeze out 1" of dough. Lift off the dough with your finger. Position on the head. Repeat if necessary.

14 For the hat: roll until smooth a ball of dough the size of a walnut. Flatten between your fingers and thumb until the dough is ¼" thick and round.

15

16

15 Cut the circle in half. Moisten the hair and position the hat. Curve each side of the brim.

16 Roll until smooth a ball of dough the size of an olive. Place on the table. Use a nutpick to make an indentation. Join to the brim with water.

Bake at 325° until hard, about 3 hours.

Ballerina

Standing on tip-toe this graceful ballerina is sure to please the little dancer in your life. After baking, use a black felt-tip pen with a fine point to draw on the ballerina's face. In addition to painting her costume, you may want to color her hair and paint on dancing slippers. Glue the dancer to a board and seal. Finishing touches include a small bow at her neck, some dried flowers in her hair and rick rack around the board. With a few changes the ballerina can become a baton twirler or skater. It's all up to you, the designer.

YOU WILL NEED:

garlic press
rolling pin
knife   1 batch of dough will
nutpick   make 6 ballerinas
aluminum foil
water

1

2

3

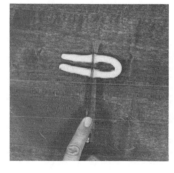

4

5

6

7

8

1 For the head: roll until smooth a lump of dough the size of a walnut.

2 Gently press between your palms until the dough is ½" thick.

   Place the head on a sheet of aluminum foil.

3 For the body: roll until smooth a ball of dough the size of a walnut. Press between your palms until it is a little thinner than the head. Pinch one end.

4 For the dress: spread water over the body. Roll out a pancake of dough 1/8" thick.

5 Shape the dress over the body. Be sure to cover the sides of the body (not the back). Trim off the excess dough. Join to the head with water.

6 For the arms: roll a coil of dough as thin as a pencil. Bring the rounded ends together. Cut so each arm is 2" long.

7 Pinch the cut ends. Dip them in water and place between the head and body. Curve the arms as pictured.

8 For the sleeves: roll out a small pancake of dough. Cut two strips, each ½" wide and 1" long. With a nutpick press along the long edge to form a ruffle.

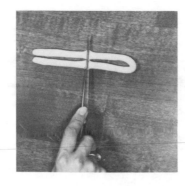

9

10

9 Put a drop of water on the back of each sleeve. Position over each shoulder. Trim any excess length.

10 For the legs: roll a coil of dough as thin as a pencil. Bring the rounded ends together. Cut so each leg is 2" long.

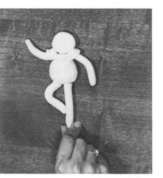

11

12

11 Dip the cut ends in water and join to the body. Gently press the toes to form a little more of a point. Position the legs.

12 For the tutu: roll out a coil of dough as thick as your thumb, about 6" long. Place on the table. With a nutpick press in a ruffle.

13

14

13 Spread water on the flat side of the tutu and position as shown. Trim any excess length.

14 For the hair: dab water on the head (not the face). Fill a garlic press with dough. Squeeze out 1½".

15

16

15 Lift off the dough with your finger. Place on one side of the head. Repeat for the other side.

16 Fill the press and squeeze out 1½" of dough. Lift off and curve to make a topknot. Place on the head.

Bake at 325° until hard, about 2½ hours.

FOIL FORM

The next four projects—Humpty Dumpty, Dragon, Hen and Chick, and Owl—use a form made of aluminum foil which is then covered with dough. This foil form enables us to make larger, thicker dough art pieces without cracking.

1   Tear off a one foot length of aluminum foil, regular weight, twelve inches wide.

1

2   *Gently* shape the foil into a loose ball — not into a hard little one.

3   Put the foil on the table. Cup your hands as shown. Gently press the foil into a teardrop shape.

2   **3**

4   The shape should be narrow at the top and full at the bottom.

5   In this side view notice the slope of the foil. Try to match it. My foil forms are about 4″ long. At the widest section they are about 3″ across and 1½″ high.

4   **5**

Humpty Dumpty

You don't need "All the king's horses and all the king's men" to put this colorful fellow together. On the back cover of this book Humpty Dumpty is done in red and blue, but any color combination can be used. The wall Humpty Dumpty is sitting on is a 1" x 2" piece of 1" thick wood. After baking, paint the wood with red acrylic paint. When dry use a black felt-tip pen with a fine point to draw on the bricks. Use the same pen to write "Humpty Dumpty" on the banner and to make the face. The fabric bow is glued on after baking and painting the dough.

YOU WILL NEED:

1" x 2" x 1" piece of wood
knife
rolling pin
nutpick
aluminum foil
water

1 batch of dough will
make 4 Humpty Dumptys

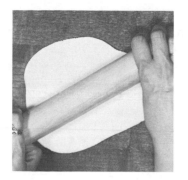

1

2

1. Make a foil form as shown on page 29. Roll out a pancake of dough ¼" thick.

2. Cover the foil form with the dough. Press the dough around the form until the shape can be seen.

3

4

3. Cut dough ½" away from the foil form. Remove the excess dough.

4. Press the ½" of dough around to the back of the form.

   Place the body on a sheet of aluminum foil.

5

6

5. For the clothing: roll out a pancake of dough 1/8" thick. Cut a line across the top.

6. Lay the pancake on the body as pictured. Trim off the excess.

7

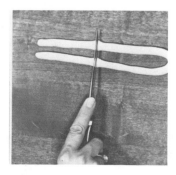

8

7. Pick up the clothing and with water moisten the back. Place it on the body. Smooth the cut edges.

8. For the arms: roll a coil of dough as thin as a pencil. Curve the ends around as shown and cut so each arm is 2" long.

9

10

9 Pinch the cut end. Spread water down the whole arm. Position as shown.

10 For the collar: roll out more dough 1/8" thick. Cut a strip ½" wide and 6" long.

11

12

11 Cut the strip in half. Dab water on the back of each strip. Place as shown, over each arm.

12 With aluminum foil cover the piece of wood that will be the wall.

13

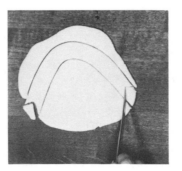

14

13 For the legs: roll out a coil of dough as thin as a pencil. Bring the ends together and cut so each leg is 2½" long.

14 Join the legs to the body with water. Slide the wall under the legs. Pinch up the feet.

15

16

15 For the hat: take a ball of dough the size of a walnut and roll until smooth. Press it over your knuckle. Pinch out a brim. Join to the head with water.

16 For the banner: roll out a pancake of dough ¼" thick. Cut a curved banner 1" wide. Trim the ends.

Bake at 325° until hard, about 1 hour for the banner, and 3 hours for Humpty Dumpty.

32

Dragon

Dragons are a particular favorite of mine—whether fearsome
fire breathers or, like this one, funny and somewhat
shy. This dragon is a bright green color but I've been
informed by a knowledgeable five-year-old that "real"
dragons are red or sometimes orange. The choice is yours.
After baking, use a black felt-tip pen to color the eyes and
glue the dragon to a board. Seal. Finishing touches include
a ribbon at the neck, rick rack around the edge of the
board, and, if you like, flowers in the hand.

YOU WILL NEED:

foil form
straw
knife
rolling pin
nutpick
aluminum foil
water

1 batch of dough will
make about 3 dragons

1 Make a foil form as shown on page 29. Roll out a pancake of dough ¼" thick.

2 For the body: cover the foil form with the pancake. Press the dough around the form until its shape can be seen clearly.

1

2

3 Cut away the excess dough leaving ½" all around.

4 Pick up the form and press the ½" around to the back of the foil.

Place the form on a sheet of aluminum foil.

3

4

5 For the head: roll until smooth a ball of dough about 2" in diameter.

6 Roll back and forth in your palms until an oval shape is formed. Join to the body with water.

5

6

7 With your finger press an indentation as shown.

8 For the nostrils: use the blunt end of a nutpick to form each hole. Make a circular motion with the nutpick to enlarge each nostril.

7

8

9

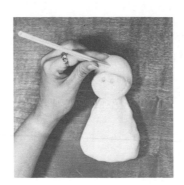

10

9 Use the sharp end of a nutpick to "stitch" on the mouth.

10 With a straw make two circles for the eyes. Notice they are close together.

11

12

11 For the ears: make a ball of dough the size of a grape. Cut it in half.

12 Pinch one end and join with water to the head. Repeat for the second ear.

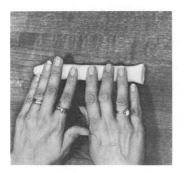

13

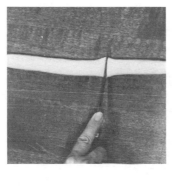

14

13 With the blunt end of a nutpick press an indentation into each ear.

14 For the tail: make a coil of dough 1" thick and 6" long.

15

16

15 Gently flatten the tail.

16 Pinch along one edge. Bring the end to a point.

17

18

17 With water join the tail to the body.

18 For the arms: roll a coil as thick as your little finger.

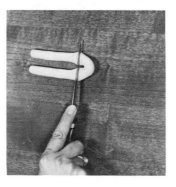

19

20

19 Bring the ends together and cut so each arm is 2" long.

20 Pinch the cut ends.

21

22

21 Spread water along one side of each arm. Position between the head and body with the hands resting on the tummy.

22 For the legs: roll a coil 1" thick. Cut each leg 2" long.

23

24

23 Pinch each cut end and join with water to the body. Curve the feet onto the belly.

24 For the toes: roll six pea-size balls of dough. Dab water on the feet. Position three balls on each foot. Pinch the top of each ball.

Bake at 325° until hard, about 3 hours.

FEATHER TOOL

The chicken and owl which follow use a new tool which you can easily make. Plastic PVC pipe is sold at most hardware stores. Buy a piece 12" long and 1" in diameter. Use a coping saw (it looks like this ⌐╖) to cut the pipe in two 6" lengths. Next, saw one piece at a 45° angle. Cut the other piece at a much sharper angle, see the diagram below. You will have made two oval cutters, one much larger than the other. Use sandpaper or a metal file to smooth the ends of each pipe. These two pipes will be used to make feathers for the hen and owl. You may find other uses as you experiment with dough art.

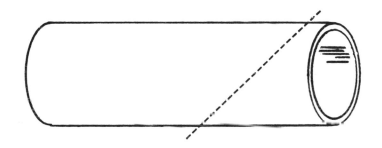

45° angle

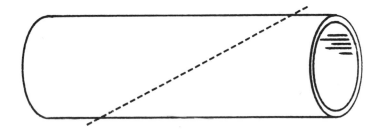

much sharper angle

Hen and Chick

Add a country touch to your kitchen or dining room with this hen and chick. Here they are nestled in a wooden box made of cedar fencing; however, they are just as nice simply glued to an old piece of wood. The nest is excelsior— try a florist or gift shop to find some. To personalize the piece make as many chicks as you have children in your own nest. If a red comb and wattle aren't to your liking or aren't right for your color scheme, paint them a rust color. The straw used to make the eyes of the hen is a very small one, a cocktail straw works best.

YOU WILL NEED:

feather tools
small straw
nutpick
lipstick cap
knife
egg yolk
aluminum foil
water

1 batch of dough will make
about 3 Hen and Chicks

38

1

2

1. For the head: take a 12" piece of aluminum foil and roll it into the size of a golf ball.

2. Roll out a pancake of dough ¼" thick. Place the foil ball in the middle. Bring the dough around the ball as shown.

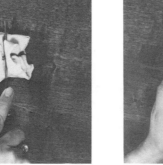

3

4

3. Cut off the excess dough.

4. Put the cut side on the table and smooth the dough over the foil ball.

5

6

5. Pinch out the cut edge as pictured.

6. Make a foil form as shown on page 29. Position the head on the foil form.

   Place the head and body on a sheet of aluminum foil.

7

8

7. For the comb: roll out a pancake of dough 1/8" thick. Cut 12 circles with a lipstick cap.

8. Overlap six of the circles. Be sure to join them with water.

9

10

9 Spread water on the top of the hen's head. Place the strip of six circles as shown.

10 Overlap the other six circles, join with water. Place on the head.

11

12

11 For the eyes: with a small straw make a circle for each eye. Notice the eyes are far apart.

12 Take a knife and make five lines around each eye. With the sharp end of a nutpick poke a hole between each line.

13

14

13 For the beak: roll until smooth a ball of dough the size of a pea. Place it on the table. Use the curved side of a nutpick and press into the center.

14 Pinch to form the beak.

15

16

15 Put a drop of water on the head and position the beak.

16 For the wattle: take a ball of dough the size of a pea. Press flat. Pinch one end.

17

18

19

20

21

22

23

24

17 Put a drop of water on the head. Place the wattle below the beak.

18 For the feathers: roll out a pancake of dough ¼" thick. Use the smaller feather tool (see page 37) to cut about 65 feathers.

19 Begin at the neck and overlap each feather as shown. Be sure to pat water on the back of each feather before it is placed.

20 On the next row, slightly overlap the first. Notice the feathers go between those on the first row (like shingles).

21 Continue row by row until the foil form is covered.

22 Begin at the left and place a row of feathers around the neck.

23 Roll out a pancake of dough ¼" thick. With the larger feather tool cut five feathers.

24 For the wings: join two feathers together with water. Place on the body.

25

26

25 For the tail: make a ball out of a 12" piece of aluminum foil. Position as shown.

26 With water join the last three feathers together. Attach them to the hen with water. Notice they rest on the foil ball.

27

28

27 For the chick: roll until smooth a ball of dough the size of a walnut. Slightly press it between your palms.

28 Pinch up the tail feathers.

29

30

29 With a knife cut the tail feathers.

30 Put water on the back of the body. Place it by the hen's wing.

31

32

31 Roll until smooth a ball of dough the size of an olive. Join with water to the body. With the sharp end of a nutpick, make the holes for the eyes.

32 Make a beak (see steps 13–15). For the wing: take a ball of dough the size of a marble. Press flat, pinch one end. Cut feathers in the other end. Join to the chick's body with water.

Paint egg yolk in the hen's eyes. Bake at 325° until hard, about 3 hours. When cool, remove the foil ball from under the tail feathers.

Owl

The neutral color of this owl blends with any color scheme. Try him in a study, kitchen, or dining room. The owl looks best when glued to a weathered piece of wood, barn board, or wood with knotholes. Any rough-textured wood adds interest to the piece. Since there is little color in the owl, a darker wood creates more of a contrast and gives a better effect. A bit of moss glued to the branch brightens the whole piece. Look for a curved branch for the owl to sit upon.

YOU WILL NEED:

rolling pin
knife
feather tools   1 batch of dough will
egg yolk   make 2 owls
egg white
aluminum foil
water

1   For the head: roll until smooth a lump of dough the size of a tennis ball.

2   Put the ball on the table and gently flatten until it is 1'' thick.

   Place the head on a sheet of aluminum foil.

1   **2**

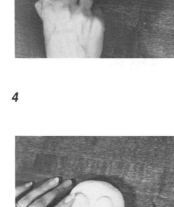

3   With the smaller feather tool (see page 37) press in the eyes.

4   For the eyelids: roll out a small pancake of dough ¼'' thick. Use the same tool to cut out two pieces.

3   **4**

5   With a knife cut a pie-shaped wedge form each eyelid.

6   Dab water on the back of each eyelid and place over the eyes.

5   **6**

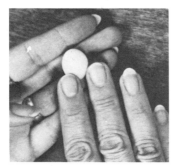

7   For the beak: roll a ball of dough the size of a grape. When smooth, gently roll to form an oval.

8   Place on the table to flatten the back. With a knife gently press a line for the mouth. Notice the mouth curves up on each side of the beak.

7   **8**

9

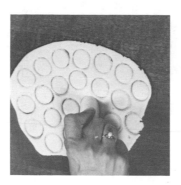

10

9 Spread water on the back of the beak and place between the eyes. Make a foil form (see page 29) and place below the head.

10 For the feathers: roll out a pancake of dough ¼" thick. With the smaller feather tool cut 25 ovals.

11

12

11 Be sure to pat water on the back of each feather before it is placed around the head. Notice each feather overlaps.

12 At the top of the head place one feather as pictured.

13

14

13 Roll a coil as thin as a pencil. Spread water on one side. Arrange it on the head, going up over the eyes. Cut off the excess length.

14 For the chest feathers: roll out a pancake of dough ¼" thick. Cut about 30 small feathers.

15

16

15 Be sure to pat water on the back of each feather as it is overlapped. Begin at the bottom of the body and make each row four or five feathers wide. Notice only the center is covered.

16 As you near the head, decrease the number of feathers in each row.

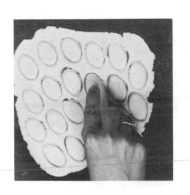

17

18

17 For the wings: roll out a pancake of dough ¼" thick. Use the larger feather tool to cut 20 ovals.

18 Begin at the lower edge of the body and overlap the feathers on each side. Remember to join each with water.

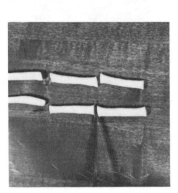

19

20

19 For the neck feathers: roll out a pancake of dough ¼" thick and cut 10 small ovals. Join with water as you overlap each feather. Be sure to cover the ends of the coil.

20 For the feet: roll out a 12" coil of dough as thin as a pencil. Cut 6 pieces each 2" long.

21

22

21 With water join 3 of the pieces together. Repeat with the other 3 pieces.

22 Tear off a 3" piece of aluminum foil and form into a coil, set aside. Dab water at the base of the owl. Position the feet. Side the foil under the feet then curve them over the top.

23

24

23 Round off the edges of the feet with water.

24 Paint egg yolk in the eyes. Dab egg white on the chest feathers.

Bake at 325° until hard, about 3 hours. Cool. Remove the foil from under the feet.

Little Lamb

This little lamb is most appealing when its wool is colored brown or black. The mouth is a bit tricky, so practice with the cut straw on a scrap piece of dough. Before baking, a tiny metal bell can be nestled into the wool under the lamb's neck. After baking, be sure to seal the dough thoroughly as described on page 10. Then a small red bow is glued just above the bell. This little lamb is a good project for groups of children, third grade and older.

YOU WILL NEED:

wire hook
garlic press
knife
nutpick
straw
aluminum foil
water

1 batch of dough will
make 10–12 little lambs

1   For the body: take a lump of dough the size of a walnut. Roll it between your palms until smooth.

2   Gently flatten the ball between your fingers.

1

2

3   For the neck: pinch one end.

   Place the body on a sheet of aluminum foil. Have the pinched end pointing left.

4   For the legs: roll a coil of dough as thin as a pencil. Place the ends together and cut so each leg is 1'' long. Repeat for a second pair of legs.

3

4

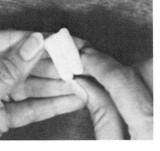
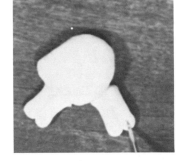

5   Join two of the legs together with water. Repeat for the other pair.

6   Dip the cut ends in water and place as shown. With a nutpick make an indentation on each foot.

5

6

7   For the wool: spread water all over the body. Fill a garlic press with dough and squeeze out ½''.

8   Use a nutpick to slide the wool off the press.

7

8

9

10

9 Starting at the outer edge, place the wool as shown.

10 Fill in the middle.

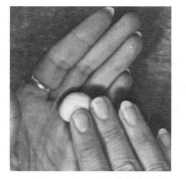

11

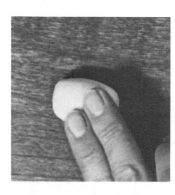

12

11 For the head: roll until smooth a ball of dough the size of a grape.

12 Form an oval by gently rolling the ball on the table.

13

14

13 Put water on the back of the head and position it on the body.

14 With the sharp end of a nutpick make the eyes. Rock the nutpick to make an elongated shape.

15

16

15 Cut a straw as shown above. Press a ⊔ shape for the mouth. Use a nutpick to make the nostrils.

16 For the ears and tail: roll three pea-size balls of dough. Flatten each between your fingers. Pinch one end of each. Join with water and place as shown. Insert a wire hook.

Bake at 325° until hard, about 2 hours.

Gingerbread Ornaments

These "gingerbread" ornaments have a timeless appeal. They add an old-fashioned look to any Christmas tree and are very easy. Make a dark brown dough with tempera paint (see page 8). Notice a lower baking temperature is recommended to prevent air bubbles from forming in the dough. After baking, use spackling paste "frosting" to decorate your ornaments. It is very important not to handle the ornaments after they have been "frosted" as the spackle may pull or fall off. Thoroughly seal the dough as soon as possible according to the directions on page 10.

YOU WILL NEED:

brown tempera paint
wire hook
rolling pin
knife
unlined paper (lined paper
  bleeds onto the dough)
pencil
scissors
aluminum foil

spackling paste
small "o" cake decorating tip
cake decorating tube

½ batch of dough will
make 15 ornaments

1

3

5

6

1 Trace the patterns on unlined paper and cut out. Or cookie cutters can be used.

2 Make a batch of dark brown dough using tempera paint. Roll out a pancake of dough ¼" thick. Place the patterns and cut out.

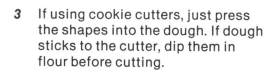

3 If using cookie cutters, just press the shapes into the dough. If dough sticks to the cutter, dip them in flour before cutting.

4 Insert a hook into the top of each ornament.

Place the ornaments on a foil covered cookie sheet.

Bake at 300° until hard, about 1 hour. Cool.

5 Use a small circular cake decorating tip (size 3 or 4). Fill a cake decorating tube (metal, paper, plastic or cloth) with spackling paste. Start by outlining each piece.

6 For special effects like the red nose on Rudolph, paint the spackle after it is dry.

GINGERBREAD PATTERNS

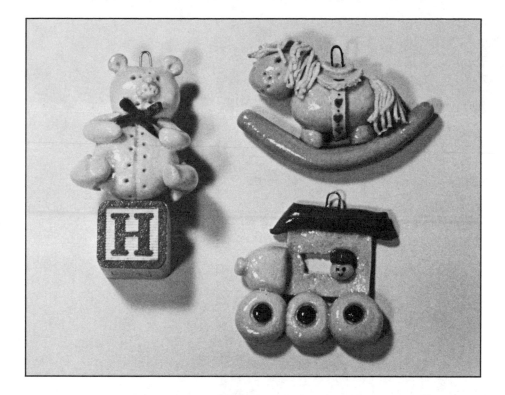

Bear On a Block,
Little Engine, Rocking Horse

These three designs may look familiar if you have my first

book, YOU CAN DOUGH IT! Here, as Christmas ornaments,

they are made smaller and somewhat simpler. By changing

the size of a dough art piece, the use may also change.

For instance, a charming mobile can be made using these

three ornaments. Also, the cowboy and ballerina, shown

earlier in this book, would work well as Christmas

ornaments. Dough art gives you many possibilities.

YOU WILL NEED:

knife
wire hook
nutpick
aluminum foil
water

horse: rolling pin
        garlic press

engine: rolling pin
        pen cap

½ batch of dough will
make 10 ornaments

1

2

BEAR ON A BLOCK

1 For the body: roll until smooth a ball of dough the size of a walnut.

2 Gently flatten the ball.

3

4

3 Slightly pinch one end for the neck.

Place the body on a sheet of aluminum foil.

4 For the head: roll until smooth a ball of dough 1'' in diameter.

5

6

5 Gently flatten. Join to the body with water.

6 Use a knife to press a line down the center of the head and body.

7

8

7 For the snout: roll a ball of dough the size of a pea.

8 Join it to the head with a drop of water. Flatten it slightly.

9

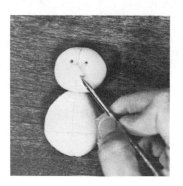

10

9 For the nose: roll a tiny ball of dough. Put a drop of water on the snout and position the nose.

10 Use the sharp end of a nutpick to make the holes for the eyes. For the mouth: "stitch" a :.·.: on the snout.

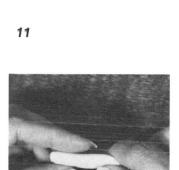

11

12

11 Then stitch along each side of the center line.

12 For the ears: roll two balls each the size of a pea. Join with water to the head. Press an indentation in each ear with the blunt end of a nutpick.

13 For the arms: roll a coil as thin as a pencil. Bring both ends together and cut so each arm is 1" long. Pinch the cut ends.

14 Spread water on one side of each arm. Place on the bear, bringing the paws onto the belly.

13

14

15

16

15 For the legs: roll a coil as thin as a pencil. Bring the ends together. Cut so each leg is 1" long. Pinch the cut ends.

16 Spread water on one side of each leg. Position the legs and pinch up each foot. Insert a hook.

Bake at 325° until hard, about 1½ hours. Cool.

Glue to a wooden block. Seal both pieces as one. Then glue a tiny bow at the neck.

1

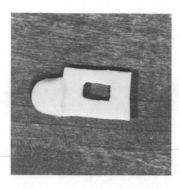

2

3

4

5

6

7

8

LITTLE ENGINE

1 Roll out a pancake of dough ¼" thick. Cut a rectangle 1" x 1½". To make the window: cut a rectangle out of the center ¼" x ¾".

Place the rectangle on a sheet of aluminum foil.

2 Roll until smooth a lump of dough the size of a marble. Gently flatten and cut in half. Put water on the cut side of one half. Join to the rectangle.

3 For the light: roll a ball of dough the size of a pea. Join with water to the front of the engine.

4 Roll a coil as thin as a pencil. Join with water to the top of the train. Cut off each end at an angle.

5 For the wheels: roll until smooth three lumps of dough each the size of a marble. Gently flatten each one. Join with water to the engine.

6 With a pen cap, press a circle inside each wheel.

7 For the head: use a ball of dough the size of a pea. Roll until smooth. Repeat for the hat. Pinch out a brim.

8 Put a drop of water on the head. Position the hat. Put another drop of water on the back of the head. Place it inside the window of the engine. Insert a hook.

Bake at 325° until hard, about 1½ hours.

Paint as shown on the back cover. Use a felt-tip pen with a fine point to draw on the face. Use a spray fix. Seal.

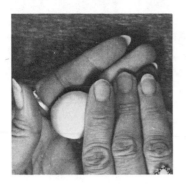

1

2

3

4

5

6

7

8

ROCKING HORSE

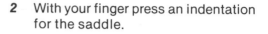

1 For the body: roll until smooth a lump of dough the size of a walnut. Place it on the table and gently flatten.

2 With your finger press an indentation for the saddle.

Place the body on a sheet of aluminum foil.

3 For the head: roll until smooth a ball of dough the size of an olive. Place on the table. Use your finger to press an indentation as shown.

4 Pinch up an ear. Attach the head to the body with a drop of water.

5 Use the sharp end of a nutpick to make one eye. "Stitch" on the mouth. Use the blunt end of a nutpick to make two nostrils.

6 For the feet: roll out a coil as thin as a pencil. Cut two pieces, each ½" long. Join them to the body with water.

7 For the rocker: roll a coil 3" long and as thin as a pencil. Join it with water to the feet. Curve as shown.

8 For the cinch: roll out a pancake of dough 1/8" thick. Cut a strip ¼" wide and 2" long. Join with water to the body.

9   **10**

9   For the blanket: roll out a pancake of dough 1/8" thick. Cut a 1" square. Join with water to the body as shown.

10   For the saddle: roll a small ball of dough until smooth. Shape into an oval. Join it with water to the blanket.

11   **12**

11   With your fingers, lift up each end of the saddle.

12   For the tail: dab water on the back of the horse. Fill a garlic press with dough. Squeeze out 1".

13   **14**

13   With dry fingers lift off the tail. Place it on the horse.

14   For the mane: spread water on the top of the head. Fill a garlic press with dough. Squeeze out 1".

15   **16**

15   With dry fingers lift off the mane. Position as shown.

16   Insert a hook into the saddle.

Bake at 325° until hard, about 2 hours.

Use a red felt-tip pen with a fine point to draw little hearts on the blanket and cinch. With a green pen make dots between the hearts. Use a spray fix. Seal.

Magnets

Magnets are popular and very easy dough art projects.
They are a great idea for bazaars or when a group project
is needed. Nearly any design can be made into a magnet—
just simplify the piece and make it smaller. The owl and
strawberry designs are smaller, simpler versions of projects
described earlier in this book. The chicken is cartoon-like
while the ice cream bar and donut are realistic. After
baking, be sure to thoroughly seal the dough as described
on page 10, under sealing Christmas ornaments. Finally,
glue a piece of magnetic strip to the back of each piece.

YOU WILL NEED:

Owl—paper clip, straw, knife, lipstick cap, pen cap, egg yolk, egg white
Strawberry—knife, rolling pin, nutpick
Chicken—nutpick, paper clip, lipstick cap, straw, garlic press,
    two black seed beads
Donut—knife, brown tempera paint
Rainbow—knife, nutpick
Ice Cream Bar—popsicle stick
FOR ALL MAGNETS—aluminum foil, water

1

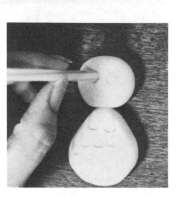

2

3

4

5

(image)

6

7

(image)

8

OWL MAGNET

1 For the body: roll until smooth a ball of dough the size of a walnut. Pinch one end for the neck.

Place the body on a sheet of aluminum foil.

2 For the feathers: open a paper clip. Press the U-shaped part along the center of the body as pictured.

3 For the head: roll until smooth a ball of dough a little smaller than for the body. Place on the table and gently flatten. Join to the body with water.

4 For the eyes: use a straw to press in two circles.

5 For the eyelids: flatten a bit of dough. Use the straw to cut two circles. With a knife, cut a pie-shaped wedge out of each circle.

6 Put a drop of water on the back of each eyelid. Place over the eyes.

7 For the beak: roll until smooth a pea-size bit of dough. Form an oval. Place on the table to flatten the back.

8 Join with water to the face. Use a knife to press in a line for the mouth. Notice the line goes up on each side of the beak.

9 Roll a coil of dough as thin as a pencil and 4" long. Spread water over the eyes and position the coil.

10 For the wings: roll out a pancake of dough 1/8" thick. Use a lipstick cap to cut 12 feathers.

9   **10**

11 Dampen the back of the feathers. Place on each side of the bird. Overlap each feather onto the next.

12 Roll out a pancake of dough 1/8" thick. With a pen cap cut 25 feathers. Join with water and position around the head.

11   **12**

13 Place more feathers along the neck of the bird.

14 For the feet: roll a coil as thin as a pencil and 6" long. Cut six pieces each 1" long. With water join three pieces together for each foot.

13   **14**

15 Dab water at the bottom of the owl. Position the feet. Curve them as shown.

16 Paint egg yolk in the eyes. Brush egg white on the breast feathers.

Bake at 325° until hard, about 1½ hours.

15   **16**

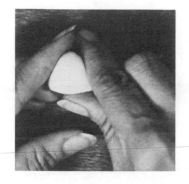

1   2

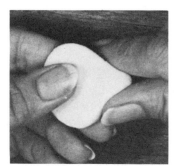

3   4

5   6

7   8

STRAWBERRY MAGNET

1 For a berry: take a lump of dough the size of a walnut. Roll until smooth. Slightly pinch one end.

2 Gently flatten the opposite end.

Place the berry on a sheet of aluminum foil.

3 Make two more berries. Join with water to the first.

4 With the curved end of a nutpick press indentations for the seeds. Notice the nutpick is flat against the berry.

5 For small leaves (the calyx): take a pea-size ball of dough. Roll until smooth. Flatten the ball between your fingers. Pinch one end.

6 Join with water to the top of the berry. Make several leaves and place as shown.

7 For the large leaves: roll until smooth a ball of dough the size of an olive. Flatten between your fingers. Pinch one end.

8 Place on the table. With a knife press in the center vein. Do not cut through the dough. Then make small cuts along the outer edges. Cut through the dough. Join with water to the berries.

Bake at 325° until hard, about 1½ hours. Cool, paint and seal.

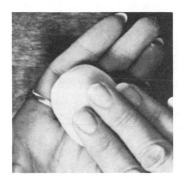

1

2

CHICKEN MAGNET

1 For the body: roll until smooth a ball of dough the size of an egg. Form an oval.

2 Place the dough on the table. Gently press until it is ½" thick.

Place the body on a sheet of aluminum foil.

3

4

3 For the feathers: open a paper clip. Press the U-shaped part into the body. Make complete rows as shown. Continue until the body is ¾ covered.

4 For the eyes: press in the blunt end of a nutpick. Take two black seed beads and press one into each eye.

5

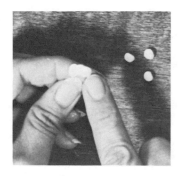

6

5 For the beak: roll until smooth a small ball of dough. Dab water on the ball. Position it beneath the eyes.

6 Press the curved end of the nutpick into the ball. Pinch both halves.

7

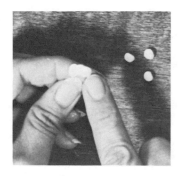

8

7 For the wattle: roll until smooth a small ball of dough. Gently press between the thumb and finger. Pinch one end. Join with water under the beak.

8 For the comb: roll out a small pancake of dough 1/8" thick. With a straw cut six circles. Join three circles with water. Notice they overlap.

9

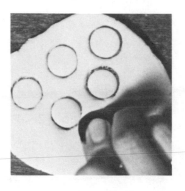

10

11

12

13

14

9 Put a drop of water on the head. Position the circles. Repeat with the other three circles.

10 For the wings: roll out a small pancake of dough 1/8" thick. With a lipstick cap cut six circles.

11 Pick up a circle. Pinch one end. Put water on the back and place on the hen as shown.

12 Repeat step 11 and place the second feather next to the first. The third wing overlaps the first two. Repeat on the other side.

13 For the nest: spread water along the bottom edge of the hen. Fill a garlic press with dough and squeeze out 1½". Lift off and arrange the nest. Repeat if necessary.

14 For the eggs: roll until smooth a pea-size ball of dough. Make it an oval. Join with water and place in the nest.

Bake at 325° until hard, about 1½ hours. Cool. Paint the beak yellow, the comb and wattle red. Seal.

DONUT

1 Roll a coil of dough as thin as your little finger. Form into a circle. Cut off the excess and join the ends with water.

Place on a sheet of aluminum foil.

Bake at 325° until hard, about 1 hour.

2 Cool. Thin brown tempera paint with water. Dip the donut into the paint. Seal.

1

2

3

4

5

1

2

3

RAINBOW

1 Colored dough is easiest to use for this project. Roll a coil of each color as thin as a pencil.

2 On a sheet of aluminum foil curve the red coil. Allow 3½'' between the ends. Put water on the inside of the red coil. Place the orange, yellow, green and blue coils. Trim off the excess dough.

3 For the heart: roll a ball of red dough the size of a grape. Flatten it between your fingers.

4 Pinch one end. Put a drop of water on the back. Position it at the end of the rainbow.

5 With the sharp end of a nutpick make an indentation as pictured.

Bake at 325° until hard, about 1½ hours. Cool. Paint if colored dough was not used. Seal.

ICE CREAM BAR

1 Roll until smooth a ball of dough the size of a walnut. Gently press between your palms until ½'' thick.

Place the dough on a sheet of aluminum foil.

2 Shape into a rectangle.

3 Insert one-half of a popsicle stick. Optional: cut or bite out a corner piece.

Bake at 325° until hard, about 1 hour. Cool, paint, and seal.

Quick and Easy Dough

This section is for the person who 1. needs a gift quickly (perhaps even tomorrow), 2. participates in a gift exchange, 3. needs items for a bazaar, 4. needs an extra "tuck-in" gift, 5. gives thank you gifts or 6. sends a little something to a teacher or a secret sister. These projects are also good for groups of adults or children to make. It might be a good idea to make up several of these pieces to keep on hand, so you will be ready the next time you need a little gift.

A special thank you to Joan Zeigler of Vancouver, Washington, for generously sharing her "Heart on a Ribbon" design.

YOU WILL NEED:

May Basket—knife, mayonnaise jar lid or regular canning lid about 2½" across, rolling pin, aluminum foil, water
Flowers on a Broom—all the above plus straw, wire, brown floral tape, needle-nose pliers, 1" wide ribbon, craft glue
Corsage—Flowers on a Broom items plus dried flowers, ½" ribbon
Heart On a Ribbon—May Basket items plus black felt-tip pen with a fine point, 1" wire ring, dried flowers, white paint, fine brush, craft glue, 1" ribbon

1

2

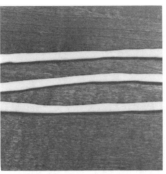

3

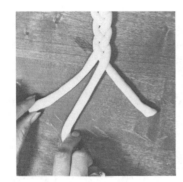

4

5

6

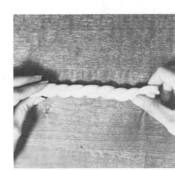

7

8

MAY BASKET

1 Find a jar lid about 2½'' across (a mayonnaise lid or regular canning lid will work). Roll out a pancake of dough ¼'' thick. Cut out one circle.

Place the dough circle on a piece of aluminum foil.

2 Take a 6'' piece of aluminum foil. Form an oval the size of an egg. Place it in the center of the circle.

3 Roll out three coils of dough each as thin as a pencil and 10'' long.

4 Place the coils side by side. Spread water along the tops. Tightly braid the coils. To braid: lift the right coil and place it between the other two, then lift the left coil and place it between the other two. Repeat.

5 Spread water on the circle. Place the braided coils on edge around the foil ball.

6 Trim off the excess braid. Join the cut ends with water.

7 For the handle: roll two coils each as thin as a pencil and 6'' long. Place side by side, dampen the tops, and twist.

8 Position the handle over the foil. Trim any excess. Join with water to the basket.

Bake at 325° until hard, about 2 hours.

When cool, remove the foil ball. Seal. Glue in dried flowers or little fabric flowers. Glue a bow at the handle.

1

2

3

4

5

6

7

8

FLOWERS ON A BROOM

1   Trace the flower pattern on this page onto unlined paper. Cut out. Roll out a pancake of dough ¼" thick. Cut three flowers. With a straw cut a hole in the center of each flower.

Place on a sheet of aluminum foil.

Bake at 325° until hard, about 45 minutes. Cool and seal.

2   Wrap a wire with floral tape. Hold the end of the wire in a pair of needle-nose pliers. Twist the pliers to form a loop in the wire.

3   Slip a dough flower on the wire. Tear off a 6" piece of floral tape. Wrap it under the flower to hold it in place. Trim the wire so it is ½" long. Repeat for the other flowers.

4   Cut off a 24" piece of 1" wide ribbon. Hold the end between thumb and finger. Pull out 3" and make a loop. Pull out 3" more and make a loop going on the opposite side of your hand. Repeat until the ribbon is gone. Lay a piece of wire in the center of the loops. Twist the wire in back of the loops.

5   Poke the wire into the broom. Twist and cut it.

6   Take a 10" piece of ribbon. Hook it behind the bow. Tie a knot and trim off the excess.

7   Glue on the dough flowers.

8   Fan out the ribbon loops. Glue in sprigs of dried flowers.

1

2

3

4

5

6

7

8

CORSAGE

1 For the flowers: trace the pattern on page 68 onto unlined paper. Cut out. Roll out a pancake of dough ¼" thick. Cut out one flower for each corsage.

Place on a sheet of aluminum foil.

2 Use a straw to cut a hole in each flower.

3 With a knife press lines in the flowers. Or, with the blunt end of a nutpick, press dots in each petal.

Bake at 325° until hard, about 45 minutes. Cool and seal.

4 Follow steps 2 and 3 on page 68. Do not trim the wire.

5 Take a few sprigs of dried flowers. Position them around the dough flower.

6 Secure the ends of the dried flowers to the wire by wrapping floral tape around both.

7 Cut a 12" piece of ribbon. Tie it around the wire stem. Make a bow. Trim the excess.

8 Curl the stem around a pencil.

1

2

HEART ON A RIBBON

1 Trace the heart pattern onto a sheet of unlined paper. Cut out. Mix colored dough. Roll out a pancake of dough ¼'' thick. Cut out a heart.

Place on a sheet of aluminum foil.

Bake at 300° until hard, about 1 hour. Cool.

2 Use a black felt-tip pen with a fine point to draw on your message. ''For a special friend'' or ''You are loved'' are other suggestions.

3 With a fine brush, paint a design around the edge of the heart with white paint.

4 Use a spray fix then seal the dough.

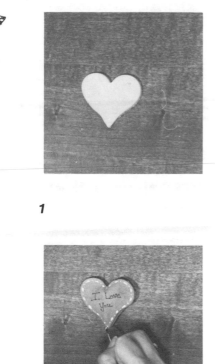

3

4

5 Cut off a 10'' piece of ribbon. Loop 1'' at the top through a wire ring. Glue as shown.

6 With another piece of ribbon, make a bow. Glue it just below the ring.

5

6

7 Spread glue on the center back of the heart. Position it on the ribbon.

8 Glue in a sprig of dried flowers on each side of the bow.

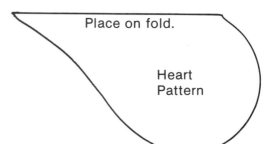

Place on fold.

Heart
Pattern

7

8

Hints When Working With Groups Of Children

Dough art is fun for kids. And, with a little guidance from you, it can be enjoyable for all. The following are some tips I have found make the process a smoother one.

1. Since painting is frustrating for many children, use colored dough whenever possible.

2. For rolling pins: cut 1" diameter wooden doweling into 10" lengths. Seal with varathane.

3. Toothpicks can replace nutpicks; however there is no substitute for a garlic press.

4. Any patterns should already be traced and cut out before the children start to work with dough.

5. Have samples of the finished product available so the group can see exactly what they are to make.

6. An adult should make the dough just before it is to be used.

7. It is better to work with small groups of children—five to eight at a time.

8. Give each child a sheet of aluminum foil. Use a felt marker to write his/her name in the upper corner.

9. When the project is made, carefully gather up the edges of the foil and fold them together to prevent the dough from drying out. Place on cookie sheets. Then before baking, unfold the foil.

10. It is best to have adults take the dough home to bake it. Chances are unbaked projects would not make it home safely in the hands of a child. Allow several hours for baking.

11. During baking, the projects will become hard at different times; check them frequently. Be sure not to overbake (burn) the projects—the kids will never forgive you!

12. Return the baked projects to school with each piece wrapped in its foil.

13. Any painting can be done within the next few weeks. Sealing should be done by an adult.

14. See the sections on "Magnets" and "Quick and Easy Dough" for other ideas.

15. Graciously accept the thank you's from the children—aren't you terrific!

Hamburger and Fries

What could be closer to any kid's heart than food! The
credit for this project goes to my son, Shawn, who made it
when he was eleven. He entered it in our county fair and
won second place. Using colored dough makes this
project easier. The hamburger has sesame seeds sprinkled
on top before it is baked. If you like, add dough art pickles,
onions, or cheese to your hamburger. As soon as the fries
are sprayed with acrylic sealer, sprinkle on salt and it will
stick as the spray dries. McDonalds® move over!

YOU WILL NEED:

knife
rolling pin
aluminum foil
water
for the hamburger: sesame seeds and dough in the following colors—
    light brown, dark brown, red, green
for the fries: unlined paper, pencil, scissors, white dough, yellow dough

1

2

3

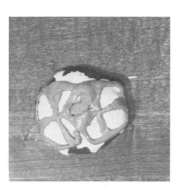

4

5

6

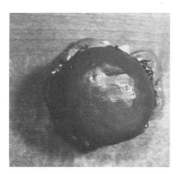

7

8

1   For the bottom bun: roll until smooth a lump of light brown dough the size of a tennis ball. Gently flatten between your palms until ½" thick.

Place the bun on a sheet of aluminum foil.

2   For the lettuce: roll out a pancake of green dough ¼" thick. Tear a ragged edge as shown. Spread water on the back. Place on the bun.

3   For tomatoes: roll out a pancake of red dough ¼" thick. Make a circle 2½" in diameter. Cut out several pie-shaped sections as pictured. Dab water on the back of the tomato and place on the lettuce. Repeat for a second slice.

4   Tear off a 12" piece of aluminum foil. Shape into a ball about 2" in diameter. With a sharp knife cut a circle into the hamburger. Do not cut completely through the bottom bun.

5   Lift out the circle of dough. Insert the foil ball.

6   For the hamburger: spread water on the tomatoes. Break off pea-size balls of dark brown dough. Gently press them into a ring around the foil ball.

7   For the top bun: take a lump of light brown dough the size of a tennis ball. Roll between your palms until smooth. Place on the table and gently flatten until 1" thick. Spread water on the flat side and position on the hamburger.

8   Spread egg white on top of the bun. Sprinkle on sesame seeds.

Baket at 325° until hard, about 3½ hours.

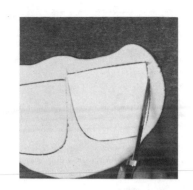

1

2

3

4

1 For the bag: trace the bag pattern on this page onto a sheet of unlined paper. Cut out. Roll out a pancake of white dough ¼" thick. Cut two bag patterns.

Place one bag on a sheet of aluminum foil.

2 For the fries: roll out a pancake of yellow dough ¼" thick. Cut strips ½" wide. You will need about 12 strips each 2" to 3" long. Cut some ends at an angle.

3 Spread water on the back of the strips. Place the strips on the bag, be sure the strips poke out of the top.

4 Spread water on the back of the remaining bag. Place it over the fries. With water smooth the edges of the bag.

Bake at 325° until hard, about 3 hours.

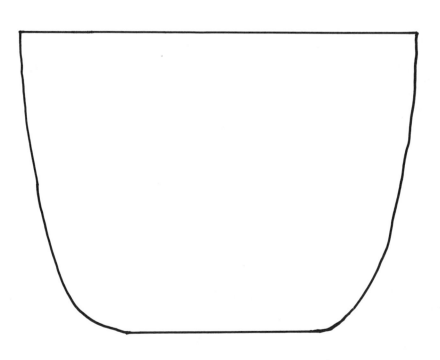

pattern A

Medal

Gifts for Father's Day often present a real problem for group leaders. This medal is one possible answer. It lets Dad know he is a winner, number one in your life. The medal pictured on the back cover was made by my son, Adam, when he was in Cub Scouts. He used blue and yellow colors, but other color combinations would be fine. The medal might also be used as awards for contests. Again, use colored dough for a bright look.

pattern D

YOU WILL NEED:

unlined paper
pencil
scissors
wire hook
rolling pin
aluminum foil
water

pattern B

pattern C

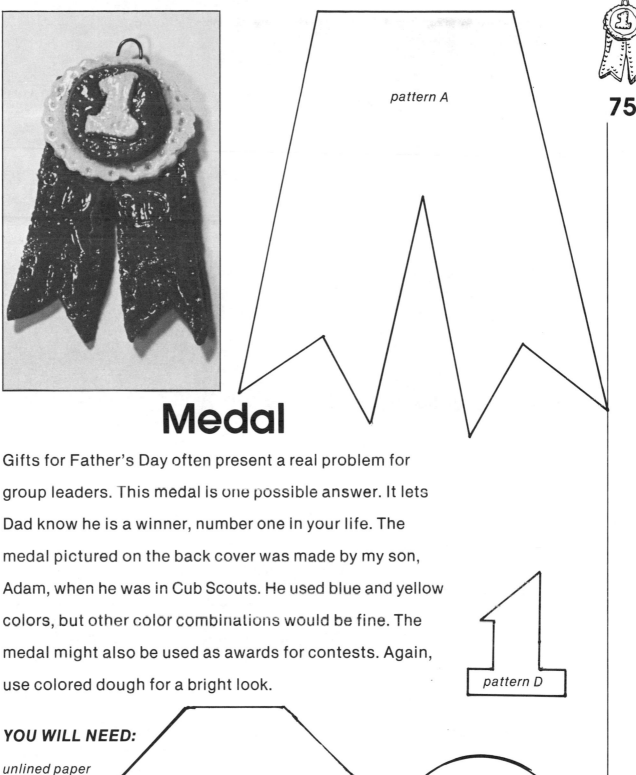

1

2

1. Trace all patterns on unlined paper and cut out.

2. Roll out a pancake of blue dough ¼" thick. Cut out patterns A and C.

3

4

3. Roll out a pancake of yellow dough ¼" thick. Cut out patterns B and D.

4. Place piece A on a sheet of aluminum foil. Use the sharp end of a nutpick to make indentations along the edges.

5

6

5. Put water on the back of piece B and place it on top of piece A. Use the blunt end of a nutpick to make circles along the outside edge of piece B.

6. Put water on the back of piece C and place it on top of piece B. With the sharp end of a nutpick make indentations around the circle.

7

8

7. Put water on the back of piece D and place it on top of piece C.

8. Insert a wire hook (half a paper clip) into the top of the medal.

Bake at 325° until hard, about 1½ hours.

Picture Frames

These picture frames are appropriate for so many gift-giving occasions—Mother's Day, Father's Day, Hanukkah, Christmas, and Valentine's Day. Since many schools have individual photographs taken of the students, these directions are for a wallet-size photo (2" x 1 ½"). Instead of paper clips for hooks, metal decorative rings may be pressed into the dough before baking. In addition to holding photographs or drawings, the frames can hold mirrors. Wrap the mirror in aluminum foil and press the unbaked frame over the mirror. Bake as usual.

YOU WILL NEED:

unlined paper
pencil
scissors
knife
wire hook
aluminum foil
water
for the oval frame: all the above plus a nutpick

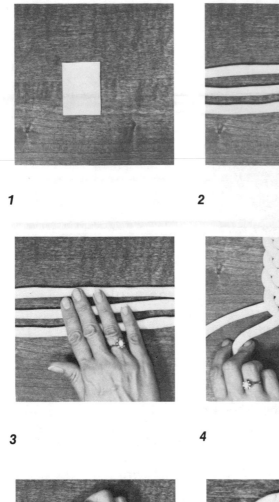

1

2

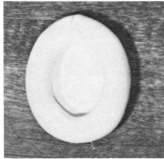

3

4

5

6

7

8

BRAIDED FRAME

1   For a pattern: put the photograph you want to use on unlined paper. Trace around it and cut out.

Place it on a sheet of aluminum foil.

2   Roll out three coils of dough each as thin as a pencil and 12" long. (If working with younger children, use two coils and twist together.)

3   Place the coils side-by-side. Spread water along the tops.

4   Braid the coils until all the dough has been used. To braid: lift the right coil and place it between the other two, then lift the left coil and place it between the other two. Repeat.

5   Lay the braid around the paper pattern. Cut off the excess length. Join the ends with water. Insert one half a paper clip for a hook.

Bake at 325° until hard, about 2½ hours. Cool and seal. Glue a ribbon at the the top.

OVAL FRAME

6   Repeat step 1. Roll out a coil of dough as thick as the teacher's thumb and 10" long. Place the coil around the paper pattern. Cut off the excess length. Join the ends with water.

7   Gently flatten the coil until it is ¾" thick.

8   For flowers: make six pea-size balls of dough. Dab water where the frame coils meet. Place the balls as shown. Use the blunt end of a nutpick to press dots into each petal. Make more flowers as desired. Insert a hook.

Bake at 325° until hard, about 2 hours.

INDEX

About the Author

Paulette McCord Jarvey grew up in Anaheim, California, and moved to Oregon in 1969. She, her husband, Mike, and two sons, Shawn, 14, and Adam, 11, live on two acres in the Canby countryside, near Portland. She started working with dough art ten years ago when she saw some pieces her younger sister had made in a high school class. In addition to teaching dough art classes for eight years, Paulette sells her dough art creations in more than a dozen stores in Oregon and Washington. She also participates in the more than 20 art and craft shows she organizes for shopping centers. Her business name is "The Dough Nut." This is Paulette's second dough art book and she plans to do another. Both books are self-published under the name Hot Off the Press.